Butterfly Gardening

How to encourage butterflies to your garden

Jenny Steel

Brambleby Books

Butterfly Gardening – How to encourage butterflies to your garden
Gardening with Nature Series
Copyright © Jenny Steel 2015

All Rights Reserved
No part of this book may be reproduced in any form
by photocopying or by any electronic or mechanical means,
including information, storage or retrieval systems,
without permission in writing from both the copyright
owner and the publisher of this book.

Jenny Steel has asserted her right under the Copyright,
Design and Patent Act, 1988, to be identified as author of this work.

A CIP catalogue record for this book is available from the British Library

ISBN 9781908241436

Published 2015 by
Brambleby Books Ltd., UK
www.bramblebybooks.co.uk

Cover design and layout by Tanya Warren, Creatix Design
Cover photo by Jenny Steel

Printed and bound by Cambrian Printers, UK
FSC and PFSC accredited

Butterfly Gardening

Essex Skipper

About the Author

Jenny Steel developed a passion for wildlife when she discovered caterpillars at the age of six and an interest in birds and wildflowers soon followed. Her mother's enthusiasm for gardening and her father's part-time occupation in journalism and photography were also instrumental in her career path. A degree in Applied Biology was followed by a Master's Degree in Plant Ecology based on her research into woodland ecosystems in Wytham Woods, Oxford University's well-studied 'outdoor laboratory'. More work in the University's Department of Plant Sciences followed and concluded with a six-year project studying arable weeds.

Jenny with plants

In 1990 she left the University to set up a wildflower nursery, providing native plants and insect-attracting cottage garden plants for wildlife gardeners. Her writing career began with regular pieces in the award-winning *Limited Edition Magazine*, a sister publication to the *Oxford Times*, and she became a regular contributor to BBC Radio Oxford. More writing work followed for a variety of publications, including *Organic Gardening Magazine*, *The Countryman*, *Spaces Magazine*, *BBC Gardens Illustrated* and *BBC Easy Gardening*. She appeared on the BBC gardening programmes *Gardener's World* and as a presenter on *How Does Your Garden Grow*.

Green-veined White feeding on Lavender

In 2005, she moved from her native Oxfordshire to South Shropshire where she and her husband have created a two-acre wildlife garden. She is a keen photographer, and her writing and images are inspired by the wildlife and countryside around her and further afield.

Preface

I grew up in Oxford where my mother tended – with great passion and skill – a tiny garden at the back of a Victorian terrace. This garden at various times housed chickens and bantams, a pond full of Great Crested Newts, borders of prize-winning Dahlias and bumblebee nests. Swifts and House Sparrows nested under the eaves and Robins in the rose arch. These early years established my interest in wildlife as an integral part of a garden, although at that time the term 'wildlife gardening' hadn't been invented.

In spite of living in the middle of a small city, my parents were both country folk, and as a family our focus was on the local countryside or the stately river that runs through Oxford's centre. It was a short walk from my home to the water meadows alongside the Thames at Iffley, in spring a swathe of Lady's Smock and Ragged Robin. As a family we made a yearly pilgrimage to Otmoor or Ducklington to see fritillary meadows full of the chequered bells of this beautiful plant together with, in my memory at least, acres of Cowslips. The Bluebell woods of the Chilterns were also a regular haunt. I grew up with all this around me but didn't at the time realise how much these walks and visits would influence my career path.

Once I had a home and garden of my own I began to appreciate how important my early gardening and wildlife experiences had been. As much as I loved the plants I was growing, my

Speckled Wood

Preface

Large Skipper

real interest was the wildlife that visited these plants, and thus encouraging birds, mammals and invertebrates into my successively larger gardens became the objective, even though this was seen as rather odd!

Encouraging butterflies to my gardens was a priority, as it appeared that there were certainly fewer of these insects around than there had been when I was a child. A lack of butterflies gave many people cause to think about what was happening to our countryside, as farming became increasingly intensive and dependent upon insecticides and herbicides. As a consequence, the flowers I learned to identify along the roadside verges of Oxfordshire and in the field margins became more and more scarce. The butterflies and other insects I was used to, especially bumblebees, suffered as a result of the lack of nectar and pollen, and soon, along with other concerned gardeners, I was growing plants in my gardens specifically to feed bees and butterflies – not just the beautiful adult butterflies I was missing but their caterpillars too that I had found so fascinating.

Gardens are now seen as refuges in their own right and together, if managed in a way sympathetic to wildlife, can go some way at least towards redressing the loss of suitable habitat in our countryside.

This book aims to provide information about the complex life cycles of some of our more familiar butterfly species, plus help you to choose suitable plants for them, and for moths too, to feed and lay their eggs on, as well as provide advice on how best to manage your garden for these beautiful insects.

Contents

CHAPTER ONE
Introduction. 13
    Why should we encourage butterflies to our gardens? 13
    Why are butterflies declining in our countryside?. 13
    Are some species increasing? What are the effects of climate change? 15
    Which types of gardens will butterflies visit? 16
    How many butterflies can you expect?. 16
    Can you introduce butterflies to your garden? 19

CHAPTER TWO
Garden Butterflies and their Life Cycles 21
    The butterfly life cycle. 21
    Migration. 22
    Why are native plants important to butterflies? 23
    What about moths?. 23
Our Commonest Garden Butterflies. 24
    Small Tortoiseshell 24
    Large and Small White 25
    Peacock. 26
    Red Admiral 27
    Brimstone. 27
    Comma. 28
    Common Blue 29
    Gatekeeper. 29
    Green-veined White 30
    Holly Blue 30
    Orange-tip 31
    Painted Lady. 32
Other Butterfly Species. 32
    The Skippers 33
    Meadow Brown 34
    Speckled Wood 34
    Ringlet. 35

CHAPTER THREE
Making your Garden butterfly friendly. 37
    Shelter. 37
    Planting a hedge for butterflies 39

Adding other plants to your hedge.................................42
Pesticides in the garden..43
Garden maintenance..45

CHAPTER FOUR
Growing Nectar Plants...49
    A general guide to butterfly nectar plants......................49
    How butterflies feed..50
    Maintenance of nectar plants...................................53
    Growing wildflowers in your borders and pots...................54
    Making a special butterfly border...............................54

CHAPTER FIVE
Growing larval Food Plants..57
    Maintenance of larval food plants..............................58
    Meadow butterflies...59
    Making a wildflower meadow...................................62
    How to sow your seed mixture..................................64
    Adding more plant species to your butterfly meadow............65

CHAPTER SIX
The Winter Garden...67
    Finding butterflies in the winter.................................67
    Helping butterflies through the winter..........................69

CHAPTER SEVEN
Moths in the Garden...71

IN CONCLUSION 73
FURTHER READING..75
FURTHER INFORMATION......................................75
    Suppliers of native seeds and plants.............................75
    Some butterfly nectar plants – native wildflowers................76
    Butterfly nectar plants – garden plants..........................77
    Some larval food plants for garden butterflies...................78
    Some meadow grasses used by butterflies......................78
    Native shrubs for a butterfly hedge..............................78
    The Garden Butterfly Year.......................................79

Small Tortoiseshell on Buddleia

Painted Lady on Buddleia

CHAPTER ONE
Introduction

Why should we encourage butterflies to our gardens?

Actively encouraging butterflies to live in our gardens by providing them with nectar plants is now an objective for a great many gardeners. In the past the idea of welcoming these insects into the garden might have seemed rather strange, especially to those who managed their gardens in a more traditional way. Most vegetable growers associate butterflies with holes in their cabbages as the rather pretty bright green caterpillars of the Large White and Small White butterflies munch their way into the leaves of all members of the Brassica family – cauliflowers, sprouts, broccoli and, of course, cabbages of all shapes and sizes. Yet, given the opportunity to learn a little more about our native butterflies, most gardeners become keen to provide a habitat for all species, including the dreaded 'Cabbage Whites'.

So what value do butterflies have in a garden habitat? The easy answer to that question is probably 'not a great deal', although a few species do pollinate some flowers for us and it could be argued that caterpillars recycle plant material. Compared to pollinators such as bumblebees or native mammals and birds that actively provide natural pest control, butterflies do not have such a positive role in our gardens, although they are, of course, a source of food for birds and other predators. Yet they are important to us in so many other ways. If lots of butterflies, both species and individuals, are present in our environment, it is usually considered an indication that there is a great variety of other creatures present also, and the general environment is relatively healthy. A lack of butterflies means a lack of biodiversity generally and we are all poorer for it.

For the majority of people the presence of butterflies in their garden is simply a pleasure in itself. All our native species are beautiful insects displaying colours ranging from bright red (Red Admiral and Small Tortoiseshell) to shades of blue (Common Blue and Holly Blue) and orange (Comma). To walk through a garden in the summer months and see a cloud of Small Tortoiseshells or Painted Ladies lift from a Buddleia bush, is one of the great joys of being a gardener.

Why are butterflies declining in our countryside?

Another reason for encouraging butterflies to our gardens is that they have declined dramatically in the wild. There are many complex reasons for this and the UK organisation Butterfly Conservation continues to study this aspect of butterfly ecology. Their research has shown that as a result of

Introduction

Small Copper

the loss of habitats such as hedgerows and hay meadows in our countryside the actual numbers of some species, for instance Small Copper and Wall Brown, have declined by more than 70 per cent in the last 100 years, plus the more recent 'State of Nature' report (see web link p.75) showed yet further declines of both butterflies and moths over the last decade.

Some of these once common butterfly species are adapting to live in our gardens and if we take their particular requirements into account they will visit and breed in this new habitat. Thus our gardens are becoming increasingly important in the conservation of some species of butterfly and moth, although there are of course species that are more specialised and will not readily adapt to garden situations. Having said that, we can do a great deal to encourage and support the ones that will and do.

Wall Brown feeding on Greater Knapweed

Introduction

Brimstone on Purple Loosestrife

Are some species increasing? What are the effects of climate change?

Although in general our native butterflies are decreasing dramatically in actual numbers, for some their range is increasing, probably as a result of climate change. Examples are the Comma, Orange-tip, Holly Blue, Small Skipper, Speckled Wood and Brimstone butterflies, whose range has increased northwards over the last 30 years or so. There is a fairly marked north-south divide where our butterfly species are concerned, and several of the species that are common in the south of the country are less likely to be seen in the north. There is very little, as gardeners, we can do about this fact of nature but the knowledge that some are extending their range is good news for those of us who live further north. However, we must balance this against the general overall decline in numbers throughout the country as a whole. There is also some evidence that butterflies, such as the Red Admiral and Painted Lady that migrate to our shores in early summer, are arriving earlier. Sadly the overall result is still a depressing realisation that loss of habitat, climate change, intensive farming and the widespread use of pesticides have all contributed to the decimation of our native populations of butterflies. Numbers of moths have also been seriously affected.

Which types of gardens will butterflies visit?

Butterflies are relatively mobile insects and will visit any garden, however small. But that visit will be fleeting if there is nothing there to tempt them to stay around, and that doesn't mean just the plants that provide the adult insects with nectar. We must also take into account the requirements of their larvae (caterpillars), including the plants they feed on, and the shelter they require. For those species that hibernate in this country, we need to think about the conditions they need to survive the winter. Chapter 2 will give you some idea of the complicated life cycle of the butterfly and how we can provide for all these different stages in a garden environment, whilst Chapter 3 shows you how to make your garden more butterfly friendly. So no matter how small your garden, it is possible to create a butterfly haven and by doing so you will be encouraging plenty of other wildlife as well.

Caterpillar of the Comma butterfly

Long winter grass provides shelter for some caterpillars

How many butterflies can you expect?

The number of butterflies you can expect to visit your garden will depend on several factors, the most important being its location and the habitats round about it. My previous garden in Oxfordshire was surrounded by other (generally wildlife-unfriendly) gardens and on one short border by arable farmland with no really good butterfly habitats for some miles around. This meant that initially this garden attracted only a few common species but was all the more exciting and challenging a space to work with because of that. Within just four years 24 species, including Marbled White and Green Hairstreak, were recorded at least in part as a result of making sure that the butterflies' requirements were met.

My current garden in south Shropshire is very rural and has woodland close by. Its position means that we have greater numbers of the 'brown' butterflies

A garden with widlflower meadows

including Meadow Brown, Wall Brown and Ringlet which can be found on the roadside verges close by, and Dark Green Fritillary visits the flowers in the wildflower meadow we have created here. So the number of species seen in the garden is slightly lower than in the previous garden (23 here as opposed to 24 in Oxfordshire), but in general the numbers of actual individual butterflies is greater, plus there is potential for several more species to find us! However, it does pay to be realistic as well as optimistic. I would love to see Marbled White butterflies here but sadly have seen none in the immediate area.

Most gardens, even small ones in built-up areas, are quite capable of attracting between 10 and 15 butterfly species. These insects have an amazing ability to search out the nectar plants they require, and if you grow good butterfly-attracting plants and have the right conditions for some butterflies to breed, they will hopefully find your garden. It is useful to know that the more types of nectar-producing plants you grow, the more species of butterfly you are likely to attract. A national survey of butterflies in gardens carried out by members of Butterfly Conservation showed that in order to attract the greatest number of butterfly

Introduction

Nectar borders for a variety of wildlife

species it was crucial to grow at least 30 different nectar plants. If you are fortunate enough to have a larger garden with room for plenty of different

Red Admiral feeding on Actaea

nectar plants you may easily attract or provide a home for over 20 species.

There are five species of butterfly that usually appear in even the smallest wildlife-friendly garden, although of course all butterflies are weather-dependant creatures. These five are the Small and Large Whites (often called the Cabbage Whites), the Small Tortoiseshell, the Red Admiral and the Peacock. These are familiar insects to most gardeners – however, it is still easy to confuse the Whites. The section of this book on page 75 has recommendations of useful books for the identification of butterflies – essential if you want to keep records of the insects you see and identify them correctly. It is also wise to know a little about the timing of the emergence of certain species or when their eggs

Introduction

Green-veined White feeding on Thrift

hatch. Most butterflies will only be seen at certain times throughout the year and this fact will help with their identification. Page 79 has information on the Garden Butterfly Year.

As well as the common five mentioned above, some gardens may also have the beautiful Brimstone, Orange-tip and Green-veined White, Holly Blue and Common Blue, Painted Lady, Comma, and some of the 'Browns'. There is more information about these species in Chapter 2.

Can you introduce butterflies to your garden?

I am sometimes asked whether it is a good idea to introduce wildlife to gardens. It is possible to buy the eggs or pupae of some certain British butterfly species and this may seem like a good idea if butterflies are scarce in your area. However, if butterflies are seen infrequently around you, it means that the conditions they require to thrive are just not available, and there is a good chance that by introducing them you would simply be condemning them to a very short life with very little chance of reproducing. It is much better to concentrate on changing those conditions by appropriate planting in your own garden to build up the habitat they require and then to let nature take its course. If you can persuade your neighbours to do the same to increase the numbers of butterfly nectar plants available, you will be well on the way to providing the conditions they need.

Rearing common butterflies (or moths) from caterpillars, though, can be a useful and fascinating exercise for small children. A 'Cabbage White' caterpillar or two from the garden, given the correct larval food plant and looked after with care, can be reared through to pupation and adult emergence, an excellent and exciting way for children to learn not just about the life cycle of these insects but also about the environment and ecology in general.

Caterpillar of the Large White butterfly

Garden Meadow in early summer

CHAPTER TWO
Garden Butterflies and their Life Cycles

The butterfly life cycle

All of us know what an adult butterfly looks like but understanding their life cycles can make a huge difference to how we manage our garden to accommodate and encourage these insects. Once I realised that the tiny caterpillar of one of my favourite butterflies, the Common Blue, spends the winter months down in the depths of tussocks of grass I thought again about how short I should cut my garden meadow areas where I knew the Common Blue was breeding. Several other species of butterfly spend the winter in their caterpillar stage, including the Small and Large Skippers.

Some, such as the Large and Small Whites, overwinter as pupae. Other species, in particular the Brimstone, Small Tortoiseshell and Comma, hibernate as adult insects. It is very important that we take these factors into consideration when making our gardens butterfly friendly, and there is more information on how to do this in Chapter 3.

The life cycle of the butterfly is something we often learn about as children. The adult butterflies mate and the female then lays her eggs on her chosen larval (caterpillar) food plants, detecting them primarily by their scent.

Hibernating Peacock butterfly

Stinging Nettles, the caterpillar food plant of several butterfly species

These food plants are very particular to each species, and some butterflies will use only one type of plant. As an example the White Admiral butterfly, which is a woodland species, lays her eggs on wild Honeysuckle upon which the caterpillars feed, and the Small Tortoiseshell caterpillar will eat only Nettles and nothing else. Some other species are a little more adaptable – the female Comma will lay her eggs on the leaves of Hops, Nettles, elm trees or occasionally other tree species, but by and large all butterflies have a small range of preferred food plants, unlike moths where some may adapt to a wide range of larval food plants. Once the caterpillar has fed and grown to reach its optimum size it will pupate. The pupa or chrysalis is tucked away out of harm's way, perhaps on a plant stem, beneath a leaf or, if the butterfly is a species that spends the winter as a pupa, this may be attached to a fence or wall or amongst a pile of logs.

When the transformation to adult butterfly has taken place two or three weeks later (or several months later if it overwinters as a pupa), the adult insect will emerge with limp, crumpled wings. Over the next few minutes the wings will be inflated with blood, allowed to stiffen and dry out in the sunshine over an hour or so, thereafter the butterfly will be off to find a mate and start the life cycle over again.

Migration

One other factor we must consider is that not all our butterflies spend their whole lives in Britain. Some migrate from warmer places and visit us to breed in the summer in a way that is similar to many species of migratory bird including warblers, swallows and martins. Examples of migrating butterflies include the Red Admiral, Painted Lady, Clouded Yellow and Large White. In general the first three species do not survive the winter

Butterfly pupa

Red Admiral feeding on *Sedum spectabile*

Lady's Smock

Peacock feeding on Lavender

with us, although in the south-west more Red Admirals are being seen in the spring suggesting that some do now overwinter there. Some of these butterflies return to the Continent each autumn, but many, after breeding here, will not survive the journey or die here.

Why are native plants important to butterflies?

Our native wildflowers, trees, shrubs and climbers are of great importance to our native wildlife. These in general are the plants upon which our wild creatures depend for food – a relationship that has built up over many thousands, perhaps millions, of years. It therefore stands to reason that the more native plants you have in your garden, the more wildlife you will attract. When encouraging butterflies to breed this is certainly the case. However, when we look at providing nectar for the adult insects rather than food for their caterpillars, there are many non-native plants that are excellent sources of energy-giving nectar. Chapter 4 has further information on growing nectar plants, but if you are looking at more than just supplying butterflies with a place to stock up on nectar and would like to provide a habitat for them to breed, you will need to consider growing their larval food plants. You will find more information on that particular aspect of butterfly gardening in Chapter 5.

What about moths?

Moths are often considered to be the poor relations of butterflies. Many people dislike these insects or indeed have a phobia of them. They may flutter around our lights at night, and we often have little more than a fleeting glimpse of what seem to be dull brown insects. But many moths are stunningly beautiful – even more attractive and colourful than some butterflies! Once you get hooked on attracting butterflies to your garden there is every chance that moths will become a fascination too.

Elephant Hawk-moth

Growing native plants will benefit these insects immensely, as the majority of moth caterpillars feed on the leaves of wildflowers, trees and shrubs. Chapter 7 will give you more information on these beautiful insects, how to attract them and how to find out what species you have around your own garden.

Our Commonest Garden Butterflies

There are some species of butterfly that we are unlikely to see in our gardens unless we are extremely lucky. For example, butterflies such as the fritillaries, White Admiral, Purple Emperor and some of the 'Blues' and skippers live in habitats that are very specific to their needs, especially where their caterpillar food plants are concerned. However, there are between 20 and 30 species that could visit your garden depending on where you live and which plants you grow. Those most likely to make an appearance in gardens are described here, although their abundance will vary from year to year depending on spring and summer weather conditions and the sources of nectar you provide for them.

Small Tortoiseshell
Aglais urticae

The Small Tortoiseshell, with its orange and black markings and pretty blue edge to the wings, is perhaps the most familiar of all our garden butterflies and one that most of us can identify. However, the loss of butterfly habitats and nectar sources has contributed to a decline in this species and indeed the majority of our butterflies, along with many invertebrates, including native bees of all kinds.

In the south of the country there are usually two generations each year of this butterfly species, but only one in the north. The adults emerge from hibernation in late March or April and feed on the early nectar of several spring flowers but in particular on Dandelions. They immediately mate, and the female lays her eggs on fresh Nettle leaves in full sun. These hatch

Small Tortoiseshell feeding on Lavender

quickly, and the caterpillars are black, mottled with tiny white spots, and have two yellow stripes along each side. They also have black spines along their backs and are usually found in large numbers within a silky tent amongst the Nettle leaves. These larvae grow quickly and then pupate, attaching themselves to a suitable leaf, head down. The pupal stage may last for up to four weeks depending on the weather, and the first brood of butterflies emerges in July. In the south of the country this life cycle is then repeated, and after emerging the second brood butterflies feed on a variety of wildflowers, especially Field Scabious, Common and Greater Knapweed, Wild Thyme and Water Mint and garden plants including Ice Plant (Sedum spectabile), Buddleia, Hebe, Michaelmas Daisy, Verbena bonariensis and Echinacea. These adults then find a safe, dry place to hibernate over the winter months.

Large White on Buddleia

Male Green-veined White feeding on *Inula hookeri*

Large and Small White, *Pieris brassicae* and *Pieris rapae*

These species are known collectively as the 'Cabbage Whites', for obvious reasons. Although they are the bane of many gardeners, they are really quite delicate and beautiful. The wings of the Large White have black tips and several black spots. This butterfly can be seen in varying numbers at almost any time throughout the spring and summer but especially during May, and then in July and August when our native bred insects are joined by an influx of migrant adults from the Continent. The female Large White lays her eggs in groups on the undersides of the leaves of any of the cabbage (Brassicaceae) family of plants, but the green caterpillars will also eat the leaves of the so-called 'Garden Nasturtium', *Tropaeolum majus*, which is distantly related. If these plants are grown near the vegetable garden the female Large White will often choose the Nasturtium leaves rather than those of cabbages and cauliflowers, plus their bright flowers are a welcome addition and attract bees and hoverflies. The adult Large White takes nectar from a range of flowers, especially Catmint, runner beans, Hyssop, Broad-leaved Everlasting Pea, Lavender, Buddleia and Aubrietia and after breeding again the second brood overwinter as pupae tucked away on a fence or tree trunk. The Small White is very similar in appearance to the Large White but is distinctly smaller and the black markings are paler. They also have two broods and are seen mainly between April and May, and again between July and September but, like the Large White, may be around our gardens at any time throughout the summer. The female lays her eggs singly on the undersides of cabbage leaves, and the pale green caterpillars are well camouflaged whilst feeding. The adults prefer nectar from Lavender, Aubretia, Purple Loosestrife and Catmint.

Peacock, *Inachis io*

The Peacock is one of our most familiar butterflies. It is mainly red with large eye spots reminiscent of those on a Peacock's tail. The adult butterflies that have survived hibernation, often in a garden shed or in a log pile, are on the wing from late March until May as soon as the weather warms up. They feed mainly on Dandelion flowers, although other spring flowers will be used. These butterflies mate and the female lays her clusters of eggs on fresh Nettle leaves. Like the Small Tortoiseshell, the female butterfly prefers plants in full sun, whilst the caterpillars that emerge from the eggs are black and spiky. The larvae grow quickly, and when they are large enough will travel to find a suitable place to pupate, often some distance from the ground. The new adults

Peacock butterfly feeding on *Sedum spectabile*

then emerge and can be seen in our gardens from late July. If the weather is favourable they may sometimes occur in huge numbers. These are the butterflies that go on to hibernate through the winter. In gardens the summer brood of Peacocks has a strong preference for the nectar of Buddleia flowers but they will also feed on thistles, Teasel, Hemp Agrimony, Ragwort, Echinacea, Echinops and Michaelmas Daisy.

Red Admiral, *Vanessa atalanta*
The Red Admiral is a stunning butterfly, its wings being almost black with red stripes and white markings on the tips. In recent years, as our climate has changed, some adults of this species now overwinter with us like the Peacock and Small Tortoiseshell, especially in the south of the country, but we generally do not see this butterfly in our gardens until late spring or early summer. These summer butterflies are individuals that have migrated across the Channel from the Continent. On arrival, the adults mate and the female lays her eggs singly on Nettle leaves. The dark-grey to black caterpillar is spiky with a few yellowish spots and feeds and pupates inside a small shelter made by sticking the edges of Nettle leaves together with silk. The early summer butterflies especially love Buddleia as a nectar source, but those that are around in the late summer and autumn are fond of Echinacea, Michaelmas Daisy and the late flowers of mature Ivy. As with the Comma, this is also a butterfly that will take the juice from rotten fruit, especially plums and pears.

Red Admiral on Japanese Anemone

As well as the five species above, most people can expect to see several other species in even quite a small garden. These are described below.

Brimstone, *Gonepteryx rhamni*
This is a familiar butterfly to most of us, although the pale female may be mistaken for a Large White as her wings do not have the bright sulphur-yellow colour of the male. However, her wings are very pale yellow rather than white and the distinctive wavy edge to the wing, which gives this butterfly the appearance of a dead leaf during hibernation, distinguishes her from the more common Large White. The Brimstone is the longest lived of all our native butterflies as it may survive for up to nine months, but it occurs only in the southern half of the country. Its distribution is strongly reflected in the availability of the larval food plants which are two species of the small Buckthorn shrub. The adult female will fly long distances to find these plants in

Male Brimstone feeding on *Primula bulleyana*

order to lay her eggs and is attracted to it mainly by its scent. The Brimstone is often one of the first butterflies out of hibernation on warm days in early spring. The green caterpillars are very well camouflaged on the leaves of buckthorn and after pupation the adult butterflies emerge in mid-summer. These individuals spend the summer and autumn months feeding on a variety of plants, especially brightly coloured flowers such as Broad-leaved Everlasting Pea, the flowers of runner beans, Buddleia and species of knapweed, as well as thistles and Teasels. This butterfly has a particularly long tongue and can take nectar from plants that other species cannot reach. These same adults hibernate through the winter months, often tucked away in a holly bush or in dense Ivy against a wall, fence or tree trunk where the leaf-like shape of their wings provides excellent camouflage from predators. They emerge in the first warm days of the following spring.

Comma, *Polygonia c-album*

The Comma is a native butterfly that was once mostly confined to the borders of Wales. Now it is widespread over the whole of England and Wales and is increasingly seen in lowland Scotland. It is the only mainly orange-coloured butterfly that commonly visits gardens, making it relatively easy to identify. However, it flies fast and sometimes high, plus it is easily disturbed and does not always obligingly stay still. When you do see it well there is no mistaking the scalloped wing edges which give the closed wings the appearance of dried, crumpled leaves, and the white comma-shaped mark on the wing underside is very distinctive. The adult butterflies hibernate through the winter amongst dry vegetation and dead leaves and emerge in spring, and after mating lay their eggs on Nettles, Hops or the leaves of Wych Elm. The caterpillars are not at all like their Small Tortoiseshell relatives in appearance but are mostly pale in colour with spines and orange markings. The summer butterflies, which tend to be more brightly coloured than

Comma on *Verbena bonariensis*

the spring individuals, take nectar from Buddleia, Echinacea and Michaelmas Daisy and, as aforementioned, like the Red Admiral, this species enjoys the juices of rotting fruit. The Comma is strongly territorial and will defend its corner vigorously, flying at any passing intruder, including the garden owner! These adults hibernate through the winter and emerge in early spring when temperatures increase.

Common Blue
Polyommatus icarus

The appearance of this beautiful little butterfly can be confusing to the amateur as the colours of both male and female are variable. The two sexes are also quite different from each other. The male is bright blue with a white margin to the upper side of his wings, but the female may be blue or brown with small orange spots along the edges of her wings. Most blue butterflies in gardens in mid-summer are likely to be Common Blue which helps with identification. This species can be encouraged into gardens by growing its preferred larval food plant, Bird's-foot Trefoil, and a few of its favourite nectar sources, especially Wild Marjoram and Cornflower. In the south, this species usually has two broods each year, with the first adults appearing in late May. They will have spent the winter as tiny caterpillars, completing their growth in the spring before pupating. On cool evenings the Common Blue can sometimes be seen roosting high up on tall grass stems, usually upside down! This small butterfly is very rarely seen

Common Blue feeding on Meadow Vetchling

on 'butterfly plants' such as Buddleia as its tongue is too short to reach the nectar in such plants. As well as Wild Marjoram and Cornflower, however, it will take nectar from the flowers of Bird's-foot Trefoil and the wildflower Common Fleabane.

Gatekeeper, *Pyronia tithonus*

Gatekeepers can be abundant in gardens that have a wildflower meadow or where native grasses are grown and left uncut. At first glance this species looks like a smaller version of the

Male Gatekeeper feeding on Corn Chamomile

Meadow Brown. Its upper wings are orange with pale brown margins and there is a prominent eyespot on the tip of the forewing. The butterfly gets the name Gatekeeper and its alternative name of Hedge Brown from its habit in the wild of patrolling hedges and gateways where bramble flowers, a favourite nectar source, are found. It is quite territorial and males will fight with each other to secure a breeding spot. There is only one brood per year. The first adult butterflies are seen in mid-July, and by late August they have usually disappeared. During the flight period they mate and the female lays her eggs on a variety of native grasses. The tiny caterpillars feed until October when they retreat to the depths of grassy tussocks and hibernate until the spring. Like the Common Blue, they then feed until they are fully grown in June. Pupation takes place and the adults emerge in July. In gardens Gatekeepers love the flowers of Wild Marjoram and this plant alone will keep them happy, although Water Mint is also favoured.

Green-veined White on Greater Knapweed

Green-veined White
Pieris napi
The Green-veined White is rather more like the Orange-tip than the 'Cabbage Whites' in its habits and preferences. It can be distinguished from the Large and Small Whites by the presence of slightly fuzzy grey lines along either side of the veins on the underside of the wings. It lays its eggs singly on Garlic Mustard and Lady's Smock (Cuckoo Flower), and the green caterpillar is well camouflaged and not easy to see. The adult butterflies are around in May and June, and again in July and August, sometimes in large numbers, when the second brood appears. These adults mate and lay eggs, the caterpillars pupate and then spend the winter in the pupal stage, emerging in late April and May. Like the Orange-tip, this butterfly takes nectar from the flowers of Honesty and Sweet Rocket but will also visit a wide range of other plants including Catmint, Thrift, Purple Loosestrife and Lavender.

Holly Blue, *Celastrina argiolus*
This strong flying little blue butterfly is found only in the south of the country and is most likely to be seen in your garden if you have Holly and Ivy, its two larval food plants, nearby. It is a species that has good and bad years in terms of numbers, and this natural cycle is thought to come about as a result of the presence of a parasitic wasp which preys on the Holly Blue caterpillars. Although the wasp clearly plays a part

Garden Butterflies and their Life Cycles

Holly Blue resting on a Borage flower

in the fortunes of this small butterfly, it is likely that there are also other factors involved. There are two broods each year, and the first adult Holly Blues are generally seen in April. These mate and lay their eggs on the tiny developing flowers of Holly or occasionally the native shrubs Dogwood or Spindle, which the caterpillars then eat. After pupation a second brood of adult butterflies appears in July and August. The females of this summer brood lay their eggs on the flowers of mature Ivy, and the tiny bright blue butterflies can sometimes be seen flying high up around the tops of trees or walls where the Ivy flowers are situated. The caterpillars that result from this brood pupate and spend the winter as tiny pupae, ready to emerge in the spring sunshine. Holly Blues take nectar from rather limited sources, but Wild Marjoram, Bugle, Water Mint and Forget-me-not are commonly visited, as are the flowers of Ivy. The adult butterfly is sometimes confused with the Common Blue but has fewer markings on the undersides of the wings, which are pale blue with small black spots.

Orange-tip
Anthocharis cardamines

The name of this beautiful little butterfly describes it perfectly as the male has bright orange tips to the ends of its forewings. We generally see just one brood a year, although in exceptional years there may be a second. The adults fly between April and June and it is a relatively easy butterfly to attract to the garden if the right plants are grown, although we rarely see it in large numbers. Both orange-tipped males and white females (which can be mistaken for Small or Green-veined Whites) have mottled green undersides to their wings, making them easy to identify when they are at rest or nectaring on their favourite plants. The loss of

Male Orange-tip on Honesty flower

31

wet meadows in our countryside, the traditional habitat of this species, resulted in its rapid decline. However, the Orange-tip quickly adapted and can now be seen on roadsides and in gardens where it finds alternative larval food plants to the Lady's Smock (Cuckoo Flower) that was the usual plant on which the female laid her eggs. On roadsides Garlic Mustard is an alternative, and Sweet Rocket and Honesty are used in gardens. The eggs are laid singly amongst the small flower stems of these plants. The caterpillars are well camouflaged as they closely resemble the plants' tiny seed pods on which they feed. They are also cannibalistic and will devour each other if they have the opportunity. After feeding, they pupate in the summer to spend the next eight or nine months in this state, deep down in vegetation until the following spring when the adults emerge. Orange-tips tend to take nectar from the flowers on which they lay their eggs, so growing Honesty, Sweet Rocket, Lady's Smock and Garlic Mustard will attract the adult butterflies and provide them with somewhere to lay their eggs. They will also nectar on a few other species, including Bluebell, bramble and Ragged Robin.

Painted Lady, *Vanessa cardui*

Like the Red Admiral, this is another migrant butterfly that reaches our shores in late spring and summer. It travels from North Africa across the Continent, making its way as far north as Scotland in good years. The adult butterfly is pale orange with black and

Painted Lady on Buddleia

white markings on the wings and is very attracted to Buddleia. Once the migrant butterflies have arrived they mate and lay their eggs on thistles, although occasionally Nettles and mallow are used. The black spiky caterpillars feed inside a tent of leaves held together with silky threads. After pupation the new brood of adults emerge in mid-summer and mingle with more African migrants which sometimes arrive in huge numbers creating an enormous influx of these beautiful butterflies. These insects breed again and after emergence feed on a variety of nectar plants including Buddleia, Scabious, Echinacea and Statice until late summer when they return to the Continent. Those that do not return die as they are not capable of surviving our winters.

Other Butterfly Species

You may be fortunate and find that you attract other species of butterfly such as Small and Large Skipper or Meadow Brown, Speckled Wood or Ringlet to your garden and the larger fritillary butterflies that feed on violets, for example Dark Green, High Brown and especially Silver Washed Fritillary. Throughout the rest of this book nectar plants and larval food plants of some of the less usual species that may visit and breed in gardens are mentioned, and the months in which they appear are included in the Garden Butterfly Year on page 79.

The Skippers

Of the eight Skipper butterfly species that live in the UK, three are regularly seen in gardens – the Large, Small, and Essex Skippers (*Ochlodes venatus* and *Thymelicus flavus* and *T. lineola*, respectively). These interesting little orange-brown butterflies have a moth-like quality to them and are most likely to visit your garden if you have a wildflower meadow or some long, uncut grasses at all times of the year. They are rather territorial insects, laying their eggs on a variety of native grasses, including Cock's-foot and Yorkshire Fog, whilst the life cycles of all three species are similar. They all have one brood per year and are on the wing through mid-summer from early June until the end of August. The males can be quite protective of their territory – basking in the sun in a prominent position one moment and chasing off potential rivals the next.

These species rely on the presence of some tall, uncut grasses if they are to successfully overwinter throughout the colder months in your garden. Both Small and Large Skippers spend these months as tiny caterpillars wrapped up in a long blade of their food plant, the wild grass Cock's-foot. The caterpillars pupate in late spring and the adults hatch in June. The Large Skipper is usually the first to appear in early June and, besides its relatively greater size compared with the other two species mentioned, the female is readily distinguished from these by the darker chequered marks on its wings. Unlike the Small and Large Skippers, the Essex Skipper overwinters as an egg that hatches in April. The small, green caterpillar feeds on native grasses, especially Cock's-foot, pupating and then hatching in July. This species is very hard to distinguish from the Small Skipper, the only obvious difference being the colour of the underside tips of the antennae (black beneath in the Essex Skipper; brown beneath in the Small Skipper; see Riley, 2007). Once confined to the south-east of England, the Essex Skipper is currently spreading throughout the south and the Midlands.

Small Skipper

In gardens the adults of these species feed from the flowers of Bird's-foot Trefoil, Clovers, Vetches and occasionally Lavender.

Meadow Brown, *Maniola jurtina*

The Meadow Brown is one of a group of butterflies that, like the Skippers, is very reliant upon our native grasses and is therefore more likely to be found in gardens where these plants are growing. Both the male and female are chocolate brown in colour with orange markings on the forewings and a single eyespot towards the tip of each forewing. The male is plainer with a less obvious tinge of orange on his wings. This species is often seen with wings closed revealing the undersides which have subtle, light brown markings. This is very much a summer butterfly with just one brood, appearing from late May onwards in the south and is in some habitats the most abundant species until mid-August. The adults mate and eggs are laid singly on the leaves on their chosen native grasses in mid-summer. The eggs hatch and the small, green caterpillars feed on grass leaves through late summer and spend the autumn and winter deep in grassy vegetation. In spring they feed again before pupating and emerging as adults in June and July. The adults of this species love the flowers of Knapweed, but will also feed on Oxeye Daisy, Scabious, Heliopsis and occasionally Hebe.

Speckled Wood, *Pararge aegeria*

The Speckled Wood is another 'brown' butterfly and, as the name suggests,

Meadow Brown

Speckled Wood

is a species that haunts the edges of woodland and other habitats that are lightly shaded. Its name also gives us a clue to its appearance as both male and female are freckled with cream or yellowish spots, some with a darker eyespot in the centre, good camouflage in the dappled woodland glades it favours. It is a territorial butterfly that is likely to spend time alongside a hedge or around trees in your garden. Both sexes bask in sunlight from a vantage point, whilst the male butterfly 'patrols' his territory and can often be seen in the same spot in your garden, ready to chase away intruders, especially rival males!

Like the Meadow Brown, the female of this species lays its eggs singly on our native grasses – in this case usually Bromes, Cock's-foot and Yorkshire Fog. The adults may be seen from late April onwards, having at least two broods per annum. They mate and lay eggs at any time between May and early October. This species has a complex life cycle as it may spend the winter either as a pupa or as a small caterpillar. The adult butterflies often feed on honeydew high in the tree tops but will visit certain flowers for nectar, including *Sedum spectabile*.

Ringlet, *Aphantopus hyperantus*
From a distance the Ringlet, another member of the 'Browns', may be confused with the Meadow Brown. They are similarly coloured with pale eye-spots and both have a fairly weak, bobbing flight, but when seen close

Ringlet feeding on Hebe 'Midsummer Beauty'

up the Ringlet is a richer chocolate brown and each wing is edged with the slenderest white border and also has a double eyespot. This species has a shorter flight time than the other Browns, only appearing in gardens with wildflower meadows or long native grass areas in July and August. After mating, the female lays her eggs on several species of meadow grasses. The eggs quickly hatch and the tiny brown caterpillars spend the next ten months in the depths of vegetation, only feeding at night and hibernating through the coldest weather. After a short pupation the adult butterflies emerge in the following July. These insects feed on a variety of wildflowers including thistles, Hemp Agrimony, vetches and bramble flowers, and in the garden will sometimes take nectar from Calendula, privet and herbs including marjoram and mint.

Mixed native hedge

CHAPTER THREE
Making your Garden butterfly friendly

We have already seen how butterflies can be very particular about their caterpillar (larval) food plants and nectar sources. These preferences are based on the relationship between plant and insect that has evolved over time and has determined the place of each species in the habitat it occupies. In the same way they have adapted to take advantage of other factors in their environment, and in order to provide them with the conditions they require in our gardens we need to look at the wild situations in which each species thrives.

Gardeners who live in the north of the UK may already be feeling a little disappointed because it is becoming clear that the natural range of some of our native species does not extend throughout the country as a whole. Most butterflies prefer bright, warm situations and are not fond of cold, windswept ones. This brings us to the first important factor that we need to consider when adapting our gardens in order to establish suitable habitats for butterflies.

Shelter

When I began to look at the butterflies in the first garden I designed specifically for wildlife there were only six or seven species seen regularly during the summer months. The garden was open and windswept to the north and east and the whole area was quite inhospitable to these insects and to other wildlife too. The area I was faced with had previously been part of a commercial fruit farm but the small, heavily pruned apple trees provided very little shelter from the wind. My first task was to plant a mixed native hedge around the whole garden and I also allowed the little fruit trees to grow and fill out. These two things helped to quickly create a more sheltered environment and two years later the number of butterfly species visiting the garden had reached fifteen. Within four years of creating the garden the butterfly count was up to twenty species and rose to twenty-four a couple of years later. The shelter the hedge provided as it grew, along with the provision of specific larval food plants and nectar-producing wildflowers and cottage garden plants, made an enormous difference in quite a short time. The shelter though was absolutely crucial as butterflies will not stay in a spot for long if it is cold and windy, however many good nectar plants there are.

Butterflies are cold-blooded insects and need the warmth of the sun to coax them into activity early in the day. They will often bask in the sun's rays first thing in the morning, and this is why making warm and sheltered hot-spots in your garden is so vital, especially in

Common Blue basking in the sunshine

the spring and autumn months when the sun is lower and less of the garden receives its warmth. On a sunny day butterflies like the same conditions that many of us do – warm sun and out of the wind – so creating more sheltered spots in your garden is a good plan for several reasons!

A mixed native hedge should always be your first choice in order to provide shelter and windbreaks and there is information below on how to create this wonderfully versatile habitat. If your garden is very open in its aspect but for some reason you are unable to plant a hedge, it will be worthwhile including a few well-positioned dense shrubs to provide at least some protection from prevailing winds. Also make sure that your fences are well maintained and gap free.

If you prefer a tidier hedge the traditional urban hedging species such as Privet, Box, Yew or Cherry Laurel all provide useful windproof barriers and even the much maligned Leyland Cypress has its virtues, although it is absolutely vital to ensure that it is regularly and diligently pruned to

A sheltered wildlife garden

keep it short, thick and under control, both from your point of view and that of all your neighbours. A tightly clipped Leyland Cypress provides dense roosting places for small birds in cold weather and may be used for nesting by some bird species including Greenfinches, Wrens and House Sparrows. Ladybirds and other invertebrates will also use it in the winter for hibernation, so it does have its uses if it is properly managed. But if you are thinking of replacing old fencing or badly overgrown Leyland Cypresses and would like your hedge to be a real feature in your garden as well as a wildlife haven, then always choose mixed native hedging. This will provide food and shelter not just for butterflies but for lots of other wildlife as well, including birds, small mammals and a large range of other invertebrates, especially moths. Planting a native hedge will also go just a little way towards replacing this diminishing rural habitat.

Planting a hedge for butterflies

To create the best sort of wildlife friendly native hedge make sure it is as wide as possible by planting two adjacent rows of shrubs. Planting two staggered rows will create a very dense and thick habitat which means it will provide a great deal of shelter and protection from the wind, but of course also means it will take up more space in your garden. If you are short of space a single row will suffice and still make an excellent wildlife habitat.

Hedging is best planted in the late autumn and winter. If the winter weather has been harsh and the ground is too frozen to plant, then very

Planting a native hedge for butterflies

early spring will suffice as long as you are prepared to look after your new plants a little more diligently. The small shrubs – often called whips – are best bought as 'bare-rooted' plants, which means they are not established in pots but dug straight out of their nursery beds. This makes them very reasonably priced and they are more likely to establish well if planted in this way outside of their growing season. The only slight disadvantage is that it is best to plant bare-rooted hedging as soon as you get the shrubs, so it is useful to prepare the ground where your hedge is going to be before buying. As a temporary measure you can 'heel' the shrubs into bare soil in the garden somewhere and water them well, but plant them in their final positions as soon as you possibly can. 'Heeling-in' means digging a good-sized hole for the roots, placing them in all together in a small bundle (or several bundles if you have bought a lot) and covering the roots well with soil. Firm them in with your feet to ensure that the roots are well covered and there are no air pockets around them. They will survive like this for two or three weeks so long as the weather is cold and they do not start to break into leaf.

Once you have the ground cleared and prepared along your hedge line, you can plant your shrubs. If you are planting a double row dig a trench about 50 cm wide and deep and add a good layer of organic compost to the bottom. The compost will not only provide nutrients for your shrubs but will help to retain soil moisture in dry weather. Plant the shrubs about 45 cm apart in two staggered rows. If you only have room to plant a single row, your trench can be a little narrower and the shrubs planted along the centre at intervals of 45 cm. After planting your hedge you can remove about one third of the top growth of the small shrubs if you wish with a sharp pair of secateurs. This won't set them back at all but will actually encourage them to branch out thickly from the base. Water them well after planting and if possible mulch along the hedge length to maintain soil moisture. You may need to continue to water for at least their first spring and summer, especially if the weather is very dry, but it will be worth the effort. Once established, a hedge of this type will grow quickly and provide an excellent habitat for small mammals including Hedgehogs, lots of bird species and a huge variety of invertebrates such as the caterpillars of a range of moth species. In addition, it will soon start to create shelter for your garden to encourage the butterflies you are hoping to attract.

The flowers of Blackthorn

Below are some suggestions of the best native species for a wildlife hedge. All of them are particularly valuable to butterflies and other wildlife.

Blackthorn, *Prunus spinosa*

Blackthorn is one of our earliest flowering native shrubs making it especially valuable for spring butterflies such as Small Tortoiseshell and Peacock plus it is visited by queen bumblebees and early honeybees. Also known as Sloe, it produces its small, tart purple fruits in the autumn. Various birds, especially the thrush family, will feed on these.

Buckthorn, *Frangula alnus* or *Rhamnus cathartica*

These two shrubs are both known as Buckthorn (*Frangula* is Alder Buckthorn and *Rhamnus* is Common Buckthorn) and both species are the caterpillar food plants of the Brimstone butterfly.

Male Brimstone on Alder Buckthorn

Dogwood, *Cornus sanguinea*

Dogwood has lovely autumn colours and can provide an alternative larval food plant for the Holly Blue butterfly which usually lays eggs on Holly and Ivy buds. The small cream flowers also attract hoverflies.

Goat Willow or Sallow, *Salix caprea*

Sallow is an excellent plant for any wildlife garden, supporting over 250 species of invertebrate – second only to the English Oak. The Pussy Willow as it is also known, flowers very early in

Wild Dogwood

the spring and provides nectar for Small Tortoiseshell and Peacock butterflies awakening from hibernation and also for a wide variety of moths. In addition several moth species including the Puss Moth and the Red Underwing lay their eggs on the sallow's leaves which are then devoured by their caterpillars. Honey bees and bumblebees feed on the pollen.

Hawthorn, *Crataegus monogyna*

This shrub provides excellent prickly shelter and food for wildlife. The dense spiky stems are perfect for protecting the nests of Blackbirds, Song Thrushes and finches, the white flowers attract a range of foraging insects, and the red berries are eaten by birds and small mammals. Several moth species also lay their eggs on Hawthorn.

Holly, *Ilex aquifolium*

Like the Hawthorn, Holly provides shelter, nectar and berries plus it is one of the larval food plants of the Holly Blue butterfly.

Wild Plum, *Prunus* spp.

The true Wild Plum is a shrub that is now rarely seen, but the hybrids and varieties that are available are all worth including in a wildlife hedge. The very early flowers provide nectar and pollen for insects, including Small Tortoiseshell and Peacock butterflies, and its prickly stems and purple fruits encourage many bird species.

Wild Privet, *Ligustrum vulgare*

Wild Privet, when left unclipped, has masses of heavily scented flowers in the summer which are an excellent nectar source for many butterflies and moths. These are followed by black berries. It is also the larval food plant of the wonderful Privet Hawk-moth caterpillar.

Adding other plants to your hedge

It is important that a native hedge is allowed to flower, as many of the plants provide nectar for early spring butterflies just out of hibernation as well as a sheltered environment for them to bask in the spring sunshine. However, this does not mean that your hedge has to become enormous. Once it is established it can be pruned

Holly Blue on Dogwood

with care in late autumn or winter by taking out long leading shoots, but leaving any berries. Keep it at a height of two metres if you are short of space or light. The native hedges around my current garden are maintained in a variety of ways. Some are now laid in the traditional local style while others are simply cut by hand or with a hedge trimmer in late winter. Here and there a Holly is left to grow to a greater height adding variety plus shelter and food for birds. All continue to flower and produce berries for wildlife, and they stay nice and thick at the bottom, providing ideal shelter for small mammals such as Bank Voles and Hedgehogs and hunting places for Weasels and Stoats. They also encourage many nesting birds as well as keeping the cold spring winds at bay.

Shelter does not have to be in the form of a native hedge of course, although clearly there are many advantages if you choose native. You can use non-native shrubs which encourage butterflies and other wildlife. Buddleias are not terribly suitable on their own as they tend to become open and straggly, but together with a mixture of Holly, Pyracantha, Berberis, *Viburnum tinus* and Escallonia for example they will make a thick butterfly-friendly hedge with flowers and berries for other wildlife. If you include a Buddleia, cut it back hard each spring to encourage flowering shoots. If you can add a native Buckthorn to a non-native hedge of this sort you may attract breeding Brimstone butterflies. You can plant climbers such as Hop,

Everlasting Pea and Honeysuckle at the base of the hedge to enhance it further, both in terms of its appearance and wildlife-friendly nature.

Even if your garden is already relatively sheltered or you have decided to plant a hedge or adapt existing features to make it even more protected, you will still need to consider some other important factors if you wish to make a really butterfly-friendly garden. The most crucial of these involves the use of chemicals in the garden.

Pesticides in the garden

If you are not currently gardening organically you will need to consider this approach if you really want to create a butterfly haven. Pesticides are designed to kill insects and other invertebrates – it is as straightforward as that. Even using those that target specific types of insect such as aphids will have a knock on effect on all the wildlife in your garden, which is undesirable. Aphids are a very important source of food for many of our smaller birds, including Blue and Great Tits, especially

Small White caterpillar

Making your Garden butterfly friendly

when they are feeding their young, so the extermination of aphids from your garden will deny tits and other bird species a large percentage of their everyday diet. There are also pesticides that target slugs, snails, ants and many of the other small creatures that form the vital backbone in a wildlife garden food chain. And of course there are pesticides that kill caterpillars, and without caterpillars we have no butterflies.

Gardening without pesticides can seem quite daunting when you first begin, but the fear that you will be overwhelmed by undesirable bugs and slugs soon disappears. As a natural balance between pest and predator builds up, as it inevitably will, it is unlikely that you will get an increase of one particular 'unwanted' creature. If this does start to happen the other wildlife that uses that creature for food will also increase in number and the balance will be restored. It is only when we take one factor out of this equation that everything starts to go awry. This prey-predator relationship exists for all the creatures in your garden. The only butterfly caterpillars that do sometimes overwhelm us are those of the Large and Small Whites which eat the leaves of Brassica (cabbage) plants. Birds and Hedgehogs will consume large quantities of these caterpillars, but there are other ways of dealing with them if they do get too numerous. They can be removed by hand and even put onto the bird table if you wish, where tits and Robins will find them. Such predation happens to the majority of them naturally anyway but is maybe not for the squeamish! Also, as we have already seen, growing Nasturtiums nearby

Nasturtium

Common Sorrel

gives the adult Large and Small White butterflies an alternative food plant on which to lay their eggs. If your cabbages and cauliflowers really do suffer, cover them with fleece when you see the first adult whites flying in the springtime. This physical barrier will prevent them from depositing their eggs on your plants and they will seek an alternative.

All the other common garden butterflies lay their eggs on plants such as Nettles, Honesty, Sweet Rocket, Wild Sorrel, Garlic Mustard and other wildflowers or grasses (see Chapter 5 for more information on this) and we really don't notice any damage from the caterpillars. In fact, the majority of butterfly larvae are very difficult to find, even when you are hunting for them.

Garden maintenance

We have already seen that only a few of our butterflies spend the winter with us hibernating as adults. The rest overwinter either as tiny caterpillars or as pupae, depending on the species. In the early autumn months the new generation of adult Painted Lady and Red Admiral butterflies may return to warmer conditions on the Continent if they can, although increasingly the Red Admiral is finding that our weather is mild enough in the south at least, for a proportion to hibernate here. So, even though we may not see the tiny caterpillars of the Common Blue or the delicate pupae of the Orange-tip deep down in tufts of grass and other vegetation in the winter, or not notice an adult Small Tortoiseshell or Brimstone hibernating in a wood pile or behind Ivy on a wall, most species of our garden butterflies are still with us in one form or another. This means that once butterflies have started to use our gardens frequently we must give some thought to the kinds of places they may spend the autumn or winter months and look after the garden accordingly.

Our first important consideration is that we have to get used to the idea of 'tidying up' our gardens much less – or not at all – in autumn and winter. This attitude benefits all our garden wildlife in a number of different ways as a wide range of creatures spend the winter months tucked away in secluded places in borders or under shrubs. Ladybirds may congregate inside hollow stems or seed heads of herbaceous plants or in the dense foliage of evergreens. In one of my gardens Hedgehogs often made hibernation nests in the borders beneath mounds of dead foliage of hardy Geraniums or under the furry leaves of Verbascum plants. By leaving dead stems, leaves and seed heads you will be providing natural food in the cold weather for seed-eating birds like Goldfinches, Greenfinches and Bullfinches. Other birds like Wrens and Robins will search out small insects amongst all this standing vegetation. Last summer's stems also give structure to the garden through the winter and provide lots of visual interest, especially after frost or snow, plus dead foliage will give protection to new shoots as spring arrives. If these areas are cut back in autumn, if all soil is exposed,

Making your Garden butterfly friendly

Ladybirds hibernating

Goldfinch feeding on Teasels heads

Ivy on a wall creating shelter for butterflies

Making your Garden butterfly friendly

if every tuft of long grass is chopped off, then the caterpillars or pupae of butterflies, as well as all those other useful invertebrates that are the backbone of a wildlife garden, will be disturbed and may not survive.

The butterfly species that overwinter as adult insects generally do so amongst dense vegetation growing against walls, and Ivy is a very important plant in this respect. They may also tuck themselves behind loose bark on tree trunks, into crevices in fence posts or creep into the depths of a log pile. Peacocks and Small Tortoiseshells especially like to seek out the shelter of a garden shed, garage or other outbuilding. They may even find their way into our houses, but any found inside in autumn or winter need to be carefully relocated to a garden shed if possible, preferably with a window slightly ajar as the spring approaches.

This all adds up to one important point. If you want your garden to be a haven for wildlife in general and butterflies in particular, do as little as possible to disturb your garden in the late autumn and winter. On a positive note, you have the perfect excuse not to go out in the cold weather to tidy up! That job is best left until early March when things are bursting into life.

Throughout the year try to keep your garden a safe place for butterflies. Think about the gardening you do, whether 'tidying' is necessary and how it might affect butterflies in every stage of their life cycle.

Peacock butterfly overwintering in an outbuilding

Uncut winter borders providing shelter

Echinacea in a cottage border sown for butterflies

CHAPTER FOUR
Growing Nectar Plants

Most books on gardening for butterflies have plans and designs for butterfly gardens or special butterfly nectar borders, but the majority of gardeners don't have the luxury of starting borders from scratch in this way. This chapter concentrates on adapting what you already have in your garden by incorporating good butterfly nectar plants into spaces in existing borders, on walls, in wilder areas, or in containers.

Most good butterfly gardens are not wildernesses governed by neglect but instead often have a 'cottage garden' feel to them. This attractive, very English style of gardening is one that many gardeners like and it is very compatible with wildlife gardening. Most existing gardens can be adapted to incorporate elements of this style by adding classic cottage garden plants that have lots of nectar and pollen, so this style of gardening is good for all sorts of pollinating insects as well as butterflies. There are also plenty of butterfly-attracting plants including some native wildflowers that are suitable for growing in containers. These will attract butterflies to patios, balconies, window boxes or tiny gardens. This means that helping our native butterflies is something anyone can do, even in the smallest outside space.

A general guide to butterfly nectar plants

In recent years garden centres and plant nurseries have taken on board the desire of many gardeners to attract wildlife to their gardens. Gardening for butterflies in particular is no longer the strange practice of a few obsessed individuals! It is now a perfectly normal way of managing one's garden. A garden alive with a variety of birds, bees and butterflies is an aim for many gardeners and this has resulted in the labelling of some species and varieties of plants in garden centres as 'butterfly plants' or 'good for pollinators'. While this is a step in the right direction, it is a rather unfortunate fact that some of this information is inaccurate. Without doubt one of the best ways of judging whether a flower is a good butterfly

Small Scabious

attractant or not is to visit gardens, keep your eyes open for butterflies, and check what they are feeding on. This can also apply to trips to your local nursery or garden centre at different times of year. Carry a small notebook with you on trips to gardens or nurseries and you will soon build up a list of plants that you know butterflies feed from.

Along with observing plants and butterflies, it also helps to know what a butterfly needs in order to access nectar from a particular plant, assuming that plant produces nectar.

How butterflies feed

Whether a butterfly feeds from a flower or not depends on two quite simple things. Firstly the flower must produce nectar in sufficient quantity to make it worthwhile for the butterfly to use up energy visiting that plant. Secondly the nectar must be accessible to that particular species of butterfly. As far as the first statement is concerned there are plants that don't produce any useful nectar at all for butterflies. These may be varieties that have been heavily 'improved' by breeding for brighter flower colour, size of bloom or number of petals – so-called 'double-flowered' forms. Sometimes this breeding process results in more petals on the flower but no nectaries which are the small organs where nectar is produced. Without nectaries there is no point in a passing butterfly visiting a flower. One very general rule to follow is that double flowered plants are often not attractive to any insects and especially not to butterflies. This is why lists of

Gatekeeper feeding on English Marigold

Female Gatekeeper feeding on Wild Marjoram

good butterfly plants may specify 'wild type' or 'true species'. However, there are no hard and fast rules where wildlife is concerned and there will always be plants that defy logic! A good example is Calendula, also called English Marigold. Many varieties of this bright flower have masses of petals, but the nectaries are still accessible to some butterfly species including Small Copper and Gatekeeper – a perfect example of why observations are more useful than 'rules'. Bees and hoverflies also love this colourful and easy-to-grow little plant.

The accessibility of the nectar to butterflies therefore is crucial. Where the flower is composed of many tiny tube-shaped flowers, and Buddleia or *Verbena bonariensis* are good examples of this type of structure, the nectar collects at the bottom of the tube until there is a nice little reservoir of sweet, sticky syrup. If the butterfly has a long enough tongue to reach the nectar, it will feed. Even daisy-type flowers such as Erigeron, Aster or the previously mentioned Calendula have this flower structure, although it is not immediately obvious. The tubes in these flowers are tiny and packed tightly together. Other examples are Echinacea (coneflower) and Scabious. If you pull apart one of these flowers you will find it is actually composed of many smaller flowers or florets. The size of these flower tubes is important. The smaller the butterfly the shorter its tongue, so tiny butterflies like the Common Blue or Small Copper are generally unable to feed on flowers such as Buddleia because the tube is too deep. They can however reach the nectar in the shorter florets of a Cornflower. It is worth remembering that butterflies, unlike some foreign moths, do not eat pollen, so flowers which have lots of accessible pollen will be excellent for bees, hoverflies, pollen beetles and some moths, but will not attract butterflies unless they also have nectar.

Comma on *Verbena bonariensis*

Erigeron with Small Tortoiseshell butterfly

Growing Nectar Plants

Peacock butterfly on an early spring Dandelion

Purple Loosestrife - a favourite nectar plant of the 'Whites'

Red Admiral feeding on Cosmos

To summarise, here are a few very general rules to help you encourage more butterflies to your nectar and pollen producing plants.

- Single flowers are usually better than doubles, but there are exceptions.
- Pale-coloured flowers and specifically mauve, purple or pink flowers are often good for butterflies.
- Flowers with an obvious tube-type structure (including daisy-type flowers) usually hold more nectar.
- Having plants that flower at different times is very important. Try to grow some that flower in spring for overwintering species like Small Tortoiseshell, Brimstone and Peacock, and others that continue into the autumn for late summer butterfly species such as Painted Lady and Red Admiral.
- Grow as many different types of nectar plants as possible. This will increase the number of butterfly species in your garden enormously.
- Flowers should be in sunny spots whenever possible.
- Flowers should be planted in blocks of one colour where possible.

Best of all when choosing plants for your borders, keep your notebook handy and jot down the names of any plants that you notice butterflies feeding from when you are at garden centres, in friends' gardens, or when you are visiting gardens that are open to the public, especially around your local area. Rely on what you see, rather than what you read. To get you started you will find a list of generally recommended butterfly nectar plants on pages 76 and 77 of this book.

Once you have started your collection of butterfly nectar plants, where should you position them? We have seen that warmth is crucial, so the sunniest spot in the garden is a good idea if you can spare it. Smaller plants such as marjoram, thyme or dwarf lavender can be planted in containers on a sunny patio if you are short of space and these will also provide you with a convenient supply of fresh herbs. Larger plants like Michaelmas Daisy or Echinacea can be added to existing borders in full sun. Try to put a few plants of the same type together – these will be more obvious to passing insects both from their scent and the splash of colour they provide. How much nectar these plants produce will depend on many factors including the weather, the type and dampness of your soil, and how much sun they get. There are several factors involved, and of course one of them is how many butterflies you actually have around in your area to begin with. If you don't see many at all have a look at the Garden Butterfly Year on page 79. It may simply be a time of year when the first brood of many species has gone, and the second has not yet emerged.

Maintenance of nectar plants

Once you have established some nectar plants you will need to think about how to look after them. The previous chapter on making your garden butterfly friendly will give you some guidelines, but there are one or two other factors to consider. Deadheading will generally keep your plants flowering for longer. Mulching with a good, home-made compost, farm yard manure or an organic mulch from the garden centre will help to keep your plants healthy and free from disease. And if you are growing plants in containers, keeping them well watered (with rain water from a water butt if possible) can prolong flowering.

Growing wildflowers in your borders and pots

Some of the best nectar plants that you can grow for butterflies are our native wildflowers and many of these can be mingled in amongst non-natives in borders or containers. Some are more vigorous than others, but choose wisely and treat them the same as you would any other plant. The list on page 76 includes some that are suitable for growing in these situations. There are plenty of good butterfly-attracting wildflowers that may be too vigorous even for an average-sized herbaceous border, so these are shown as suitable for a 'wild patch'.

Making a special butterfly border

If you have lots of space in your garden or you are designing a garden from scratch, you can of course make a special butterfly border using a mixture of the recommended plants in the list on pages 76 and 77 and from the notes you have made while visiting other gardens. Choose a warm sunny spot in your garden if you can and prepare the soil thoroughly by removing perennial weeds and adding organic compost. Select some shrubs from your list for the very back to give height and shelter, and then intermingle a selection of wildflowers, cottage garden plants and herbs in the area in front of the shrubs, placing the taller plants towards the back, although I like to have the occasional tall plant towards the front for a little variety in shape. There is really no great mystery to designing a border like this. You can think a little bit about the colours you like and place plants with those flower colours next to each other to create some areas where the hues blend together, or go for extreme contrasts like purple next to yellow. Include plants that flower in the spring, summer and into the autumn and, if you like, add a few caterpillar food plants selected from those listed in the next chapter.

As far as looking after your border is concerned, disturb it as little as possible in the autumn and winter, and cut back dead growth and prune Buddleias hard in early spring. You can mulch after cutting back when the soil is damp – this will suppress weeds and conserve water as well as feed the plants, keeping them healthy and strong.

Growing Nectar Plants

A sheltered butterfly border

Bird's-foot Trefoil and Common Blue

CHAPTER FIVE
Growing larval Food Plants

The plants on which our butterflies and moths lay their eggs are known as their larval or caterpillar food plants, and the leaves or sometimes the flower buds or seed pods of these plants are eaten by the caterpillars when they hatch from the carefully positioned eggs. In general these plants are native flowers or shrubs as you would expect, but some of our butterflies have adapted to laying their eggs on non-native plants which are similar to those they normally use. An example of a versatile butterfly is the Orange-tip. The female of this species normally uses the leaves of Lady's Smock (sometimes called Cuckoo Flower) for her caterpillars but is also happy to lay her eggs on

The tiny egg of an Orange-tip butterfly on an Honesty flower

Honesty or Sweet Rocket, both are plants from the same family as Lady's Smock but not native to Britain. These alternative plants are very useful to the butterfly gardener as they are very attractive garden flowers in their own right and add greatly to a colourful spring garden. In the list of larval food plants on page 78, those that are not native are indicated.

The majority of our butterflies' larval food plants though are native plants and, assuming that we wish butterflies to breed in our gardens, and this is perhaps the most practical way that gardeners can contribute to their conservation, we need to be able to incorporate these food plants into the garden in an attractive way. Some are perfect in borders or even containers (the golden-flowered Bird's-foot Trefoil for the Common Blue is a good example of a species suitable for pots) and can be grown in quite small gardens, whereas others like the less colourful Garlic Mustard, can be tucked into the bottom of a hedge where it will establish and self seed. I tend to allow several of these caterpillar food plants to seed and spread wherever they want to in my garden because the more opportunities there are for butterflies to breed, the more adults I will have flying around the garden feeding on the summer flowers in my borders. The list on page 78 gives

57

Growing larval Food Plants

Caterpillars of the Peacock butterfly on Nettles

Garlic Mustard, the larval food plant of the Orange-tip butterfly.

Orange-tip caterpillar

an idea of some good locations for these essential plants and it is useful to remember that for most a sunny spot is necessary.

Maintenance of larval food plants

The maintenance of these plants is crucial. There is obviously no point in growing them only to snip off the vital bits when the eggs have been laid, the caterpillars are feeding on them, or the pupae are attached to the leaves or stems, and generally you won't be able to find eggs, larvae or pupae because they are very well camouflaged.
The only exceptions are the very conspicuous Small Tortoiseshell and Peacock larvae. These spiky, black caterpillars can be quite obvious on the leaves of Nettles as they are usually massed together in a tent of silken threads.

So on the whole maintenance is simply a question of leaving these plants alone as much as possible and only tidying them up a little, if at all, in the early spring along with your nectar plants. Don't be tempted to pull out Sweet Rocket, Honesty or Garlic Mustard when they are setting seed as caterpillars of the Orange-tip or Green-veined White butterflies could be hiding amongst the seed pods which they closely resemble. The only active maintenance you need to consider is to cut back Nettles if you want to grow them in your garden, in late June or early July, first checking that there are no caterpillars. Once the first broods of Peacock and Small Tortoiseshell caterpillars have gone through their life cycle and the new butterflies are on the wing, this next generation of adults prefers to lay its eggs on fresh young Nettle leaves, which will spring up if you cut the plants back at this time.

Meadow butterflies

It is relatively easy in most gardens to attract a selection of our larger, most colourful butterfly species. Painted Lady, Small Tortoiseshell, Comma, Brimstone, Red Admiral and Peacock will all feed on nectar plants, especially Buddleia, that we can provide for them, and with some thoughtful planting we can also tempt them to breed by including their larval food plants in our gardens. In some locations there may be a few other large, colourful species that we may see, like the migrant Clouded Yellow that may appear in

A garden wildflower meadow for butterflies

warm summers. I am fortunate to live near a wood where Dark Green Fritillaries breed and these gorgeous butterflies come to feed on the Knapweed in my wildflower meadow.

Clouded Yellow on Common Knapweed

Dark Green Fritillary on Common Knapweed

Growing larval Food Plants

Butterflies from top
Left: **Gatekeeper, Speckled Wood, Marbled White**. Right: **Ringlet, Meadow Brown, Wall Brown**

Growing larval Food Plants

Small Skipper

Male Large Skipper

But so far there is one group of butterflies that we haven't mentioned. These are the species that lay their eggs on native grasses, often in meadows or perhaps on the grasses on the sunny side of a hedgerow. The life cycles and food preferences of these butterfly species indicate how important long, undisturbed grass is to these insects in the countryside. But with the right conditions, some of them can be encouraged to our gardens to breed and stay around if we supply them with their larval food plants – native grasses. They include the Gatekeeper, Speckled Wood, Marbled White, Ringlet, Meadow Brown, Small and Large Skipper, Small Heath and Wall Brown. This sounds like a gardener's dream – caterpillars that keep the grass short for us! But sadly this is not quite the situation. They do eat the leaves of some of our native grass species, but once again you would hardly notice their presence. These are meadow butterflies that have very specific breeding requirements and one of these is that the grasses they lay their eggs on must be kept relatively long and undisturbed. The other important consideration is that the average rye grass lawn will not do. The best way of making a home for these butterfly species is to create a wildflower meadow containing a selection of several different species of native grass.

Native meadow grasses

Making a wildflower meadow

Wildflower meadows have become very popular in recent years, in both large and small gardens. They look wonderful, can reduce the amount of work in the garden and, of course, attract a wide range of wildlife – not just the butterflies that are the focus of this book but invertebrates of all types, including dragonflies and damselflies that rest amongst the long grasses, bees that feed from the flowers and mammals, especially voles and shrews plus amphibians, reptiles and birds. They are perfect wildlife habitats.

Garden meadows should always be created in full sun whenever possible. Although you can create an area of wildflowers and grass in light shade, for instance under fruit trees, we have already seen that butterflies are more likely to be attracted to the sunnier spots in your garden. It is important to consider your soil type before you embark on a project such as a meadow. In deep, fertile soil a meadow will not establish well as the grass will grow too vigorously and swamp the wildflowers. There should preferably be no perennial weeds such as thistles or couch grass, although thistles in a little wild patch can be good butterfly nectar plants. So thought and preparation are needed and there could be some hard work ahead.

If you feel you have a suitable spot for a wildflower meadow, the area must first be prepared. If there is turf, it must be stripped off, unless it is very thin, patchy and composed of native species. If you think this might be the case, it is best to research more information about making meadows (i.e. see *Making Garden Meadows*, the first book in the series Gardening with Nature) and follow directions for enhancing an existing grassy area. It is worth bearing in mind that it is very difficult to convert a modern rye grass lawn into a wildflower meadow. The best you may be able to do is add spring bulbs which should cope with growing amongst the tough rye grass.

In the case of your potential meadow spot having existing grass, you may need to hire a turf cutter if the area is large. If your soil is very fertile, it may be necessary to remove the top layer

Wildflower meadow with Common Spotted Orchids

of soil and replace with something poorer – the soil from the bottom of a hole where a pond is to be installed is often ideal. If you are removing turf from an area where the grass has been neglected, never fertilised but repeatedly mown year after year, then the soil quality should be suitable for a garden meadow.

When converting an area where there is no grass your first task is to remove any perennial weeds. For small areas digging out thistle, Nettle, Ground Elder and Couch Grass roots is the organic alternative. If you can think well ahead, covering the area with thick black polythene to exclude light for a few months will also achieve the desired result. It is best to avoid using any herbicides (or pesticides) in a wildlife garden.

The best time to sow a wildflower meadow seed mixture is very early spring, but autumn can also produce a good result. There are several specialist seed growers producing native grass and wildflower mixes (see Further Information page 75), and it is vital to ensure that the seeds are of native origin. It is also important to choose a mixture that suits your particular soil. Do you have clay or sand or chalky soil? Is it well drained or waterlogged? Wildflowers can be very fussy about the soil conditions they prefer and if you plant inappropriate species for your soil type they may not germinate or may quickly disappear. Your seed

Bumblebee feeding on Knapweed

supplier will have a range of mixes suitable for all soil types. You will need to roughly calculate the area you have and sow a seed mixture at a rate of about 4 gm per square metre.

How to sow your seed mixture

Hopefully you now have soil that is weed-free and not too fertile. It should be broken down into a fine tilth, and the seed scattered onto the soil surface as evenly as possible. The best course of action is to then walk up and down on the area, pressing the seed into the soil with your feet or you can use a garden roller. It is not necessary to cover the seed up – in fact excluding light can hinder germination of some native wildflowers so leave it uncovered but simply pressed down as best you can. When sowing is complete, water well if the conditions are dry and protect the seed from birds. The most effective way of doing this is to hang a few old, shiny CDs or DVDs around the area to sparkle and catch the light. This always seems to work really well in my garden, and I have lots of finches around. Covering your meadow seed with netting is never a good option as birds or even small mammals, including Hedgehogs, can get tangled up in it.

The grasses will germinate first depending on the weather conditions and some of the wildflower species could also appear quite quickly. Others, especially Cowslips, will not germinate until they have had a period of cold frosty weather, so if you sow in the springtime you may not see these until

Bird's-foot Trefoil

the following year. Over time new species will appear and you can also expect some germination of seeds that have lain dormant, sometimes for many years, in your own soil.

Your meadow will need basic annual maintenance. It must be cut at least once every year in late summer or autumn, and the hay raked off thoroughly in order to maintain the conditions that the wildflowers require. But you must ensure that the grass is not cut too short or you may be exposing the butterfly caterpillars and pupae that could be resting down in the short turf over the winter months. In general, cutting your meadow to between 5 and 10cm will keep these insects safe from the worst of the weather and from predators, although of course a certain amount of predation from birds, hedgehogs and other insects is quite natural and must be expected.

If you are a real enthusiast your meadow maintenance can be much more complicated. Parts of the meadow can be cut at different times to encourage particular butterfly species to breed, but in general the keen gardener can contribute to the breeding success of the meadow butterflies with just the basic upkeep outlined above.

Adding more plant species to your butterfly meadow

So long as you have sown a seed mixture from a reputable supplier, it will contain the essential grass species for some of our meadow butterflies such as Ringlet and Meadow Brown. If you have any doubt check the list of species in your seed mix with the list of larval food plants on page 78. If the specific types of grass are not included, go to another supplier. One useful addition you can make to your meadow once it is established is to add small plants or plugs of other larval food plants or special nectar plants to really give your local butterflies plenty of options. I always try to add extra larval food plants when making a wildflower meadow, especially Bird's-foot Trefoil for the Common Blue, Sheep's Sorrel for the Small Copper, and then a few more good nectar plants for the adults – Common and Greater Knapweed in particular which attract a wide range of butterfly species. A damp clay soil will also be good for Lady's Smock which will provide a larval food plant and nectar source for the Orange-tip butterfly. These extra species can make a meadow look a bit 'top heavy' with flowers compared to a traditional hay meadow, but the objective is to make a

Female Large White feeding on Greater Knapweed

good habitat for butterflies rather than try to recreate a proper wild meadow. What you are doing here is making a 'meadow effect' in your garden and if you want it to have lots of flowers it's up to you!

If you have decided that a small meadow in your garden is something you would like to try, make sure you read the information on making meadows in one of the books recommended on page 75 in Further Reading.

So it is quite possible for the average gardener to contribute to the survival of some of our prettiest butterflies by catering for their caterpillars' needs in the garden. With some larval food plants in your borders or containers, maybe a little meadow area in a sunny spot, combined with appropriate garden maintenance, you will find that both the numbers of individuals and species of butterfly in your garden will start to increase.

Shelter in the winter garden

CHAPTER SIX
The Winter Garden

Throughout this book the overwintering of butterflies has been frequently mentioned and it stands to reason that if we want these insects to be with us year after year they must get through the cold winter months in some form or another. As we have already seen, a few species hibernate as adult butterflies and most of us have come across a Peacock or Small Tortoiseshell butterfly flapping against the window of a garden shed or garage on a mild and sunny winter's day. Some survive the winter as tiny caterpillars, waiting for warmer weather before they continue to feed on their larval food plant. Others spend the winter as pupae in suspended animation. These butterflies emerge as fully grown adults in spring when the conditions are right for them.

Finding butterflies in the winter

We are unlikely to see a caterpillar or pupa outside during the winter months – they are usually tucked away safely and are difficult to find. As long as the garden is not over tidied, they will be safe and can be left to themselves. We can be more positively helpful to the species that overwinter as adults by providing them with shelter. Firstly though, what should we do with a butterfly in a garage or shed on a sunny winter's day? If the weather is relatively warm early in the year a butterfly can be let out to find a new, more suitable hibernation place. Sometimes butterflies find their way into the house in the autumn and choose an out-of-the-way spot in a bedroom or other cool room for hibernation. They may wake up because the room warms up. Putting them outside in freezing weather would almost certainly finish them off. In this situation it is best to relocate them to a cool but frost-free shed or garage where hopefully they will return to hibernation unharmed. Unfortunately, any butterfly coming out of hibernation early has a problem in that it will have used up some of its stored food reserves, and there will be very little or no nectar around for it outside. The more good hibernation places you have outside for butterflies, the less likely they are to come into

Small Tortoiseshell waking from hibernation

Dandelion – the best early nectar plant for butterflies

A garden log pile, providing shelter for hibernating butterflies

the house and find themselves in this situation. They are adept at finding dry places in log piles, under flakes of bark on tree stumps, in the overlap in larch lap fencing or sometimes in cracks in walls. One of the best hibernation spots for adult butterflies, especially the Brimstone and Comma, is amongst climbing vegetation on walls. Ivy is particularly good for this purpose.

Below are a few ideas on how to help your butterflies through the winter months.

Helping butterflies through the winter

- Make sure you have early flowering nectar plants, especially Dandelions.
- Leave Ivy and other thick climbing plants against walls or tree trunks undisturbed.
- Create log piles or twig piles and leave dead tree stumps with flaking bark.
- Leave all herbaceous plants alone until early spring.
- Cut meadows in the autumn to no less that 5cm and then leave undisturbed through the winter.
- Try to leave a few small areas of long grass completely uncut through the autumn and winter and cut them in the springtime.

These measures will help all sorts of wildlife in your garden, not just butterflies.

Herbaceous nectar borders left uncut through the winter

Moth caterpillars – from top: Left: **Angle Shades, Five-spot Burnet, Elephant Hawk-moth, Grey Dagger.**
Right: **Drinker, Mullein Moth, Poplar Hawk-moth**

CHAPTER SEVEN
Moths in the Garden

As a small child I became fascinated with the caterpillars of moths. Caterpillars are wonderful creepy-crawlies that are easy to find and could be fed and looked after until they pupated and emerged into the adult insect. I discovered that many had stunningly coloured wings with beautiful symmetrical patterns and soft, furry antennae. I successfully reared a Privet Hawk-moth caterpillar (found walking across the garden path) and watched it feed and grow, bury itself into the soil in the bottom of the large container that was its home, and then hatch as a gorgeous fully-fledged adult. Other less exotic species also joined my little caterpillar farm, each one identified and carefully researched as to its larval food plant, although generally this could often be easily determined by knowing the name of the plant on which I found it. I took great delight in releasing the adults back into the wild. Many years on, moths are still a great passion and I regularly run a 'moth trap' overnight in my garden and identify and catalogue the species that I find.

Gardening for moths is not something that automatically comes to mind for many gardeners, but these wonderful insects are in decline in just the same way that many butterflies are (see 'Moths Decline' on Butterfly Conservation Website). Loss of

Privet Hawk-moth

habitat and larval food plants is just as devastating a problem for moths as it is for the butterflies we want to see in our gardens. The good news is that many of the plants that provide nectar for butterflies are also favoured by moths. However, it is also quite easy to grow the larval food plants of some moths as they tend to have less fastidious tastes than our native butterflies. The caterpillars of many moth species will feed on a variety of plants and are less specific about these than butterflies tend to be. Some have a range of tree or shrub leaves on which the caterpillars feed and it is relatively easy to make sure certain of these plants are included in the garden. Most of these larval food plants are native wildflowers and many are easy to grow alongside a hedge or in a small wildflower meadow. You will find a list of some of the most versatile of these larval food plants on page 78.

Goat Willow catkins

Not all adult moths feed in the same way that butterflies do. As mentioned earlier, some feed on pollen as well as nectar, but others don't feed at all during their short lives. But managing your garden for butterflies in the way described in Chapter 5 will also make it a better place for moths whether they require nectar or not. Many moths overwinter as pupae or caterpillars in just the same way that some butterflies do, often buried in the soil and in leaf litter. Leaving a patch of long grass somewhere in the garden that is undisturbed by trampling feet will encourage several species like Large Yellow Underwing and Dark Arches to survive in this state until the spring. A willow of some description, especially Sallow (Goat Willow), *Salix caprea*, will provide food for the caterpillars of many species, and a native hedge will also provide food for many caterpillars.

Discovering the mysterious world of the moths that use your garden is an exciting extension of gardening

Micro-moth, *Adela reaumurella*

Hummingbird Hawk-moth feeding on Buddleia

Six-spot Burnet Moth

for butterflies. Our native species (of which there are around 2500, including the 'micro-moths') are an incredibly important part of the natural food chain and some bird species, especially the tits, are heavily reliant on the caterpillars of moths to feed their young in the spring. By managing your garden for butterflies in the ways described in the previous chapters, moths will also naturally benefit. Grow Buddleia and Lavender for nectar plus a range of native wildflowers such as Bird's-foot Trefoil, bedstraws, native grasses and shrubs and you will have a garden where many species of moth will thrive.

In Conclusion

Butterflies and moths can enhance our enjoyment of gardens tremendously. Even the most beautiful garden devoid of these lovely colourful insects will seem less interesting and alive. As we continue to lose good butterfly habitat from our countryside, anyone with a garden, however small, can make a really valuable contribution to the conservation of some of our native species by creating a habitat for them in their own little nature reserve outside the back door. Grow some of the plants

Large Skipper

they need, provide them with shelter throughout the year and they, and all the other wildlife visiting your garden, will benefit.

Meadow Brown on Knapweed flower

Further Reading

Steel, J. (2013) *Making Garden Meadows*, Brambleby Books.

Steel, J. (2006) *Bringing a Garden to Life*, Wiggly Wigglers.

Riley, A.M. (2007) *British and Irish Butterflies*, Brambleby Books.

Thomas, A. (2010) *Gardening for Wildlife – A Complete Guide to Nature-friendly Gardening.* A & C Black, London.

Lewington, R. (2015) *Pocket Guide to the Butterflies of Great Britain and Ireland.* British Wildlife Publishing.

Waring P., Townsend M. and Lewington R. (2009) *Field Guide to the Moths of Great Britain and Ireland.* British Wildlife Publishing.

RSPB (2013) State of Nature, http://www.rspb.org.uk/Images/stateofnature_tcm9-345839.pdf

Websites:

Butterfly Conservation: www.butterfly-conservation.org

UK Butterflies: www.ukbutterflies.co.uk

State of Nature: www.rspb.org.uk/Images/stateofnature_tcm9-345839.pdf, 2013

Further Information

Suppliers of native seeds and plants

Emorsgate Seeds: Limes Farm, Tilney All Saints, Kings Lynn, Norfolk PE34 4RT,
Tel: 01553 829028
www.wildseed.co.uk

Habitataid: Hookgate Cottage, South Brewham, Somerset BA10 0LQ,
Tel: 01749 812355
www.habitataid.co.uk

Chiltern Seeds Ltd: Crowmarsh Battle Barns, 114 Preston Crowmarsh, Wallingford, OX10 6SL,
Tel. 01491 824675
www.chilternseeds.co.uk

Jenny Steel's website www.wildlife-gardening.co.uk has a complete guide to wildlife gardening, including updated lists of suppliers.

Some butterfly nectar plants – native wildflowers

Wildflower	Colour/Flowering Time	Add to	Favourite nectar source for..
Betony	Pink/June-October	Border, meadow	Brimstone
Bird's-foot Trefoil	Yellow/June-September	Border, container, meadow	Common Blue, Skippers
Bluebell	Blue/April-June	Shady border or grass	Brimstone, Large White
Bramble	White/May-November	Hedgerow, wild patch	Many species
Broad-leaved Pea	Pink/July-August	Border, patio	Brimstone, Large White
Bugle	Purple/April-June	Border, pond edge, container	Whites
Burdock	Pink/July-September	Wild patch	Peacock, Small Tortoiseshell
Common Fleabane	Yellow/August-September	Border, pond edge	Many species
Common Knapweed	Purple/June-September	Meadow	Many species
Common Valerian	Pink/June-August	Border, pond edge	Small Tortoiseshell
Cornflower	Blue/June-August	Border, container	Common Blue, Gatekeeper
Corn Marigold	Yellow/June-August	Border, container	Skippers
Creeping Thistle	Purple/June-September	Wild patch	Small Tortoiseshell
Creeping Thyme	Pink/May-August	Border, container	Many species
Dandelion	Yellow/March-October	Meadow	Many species
Field Scabious	Mauve/July-September	Border, meadow	Many species
Garlic Mustard	White/April-June	Border, shady grass	Orange-tip, Green-veined White
Greater Bird's-foot Trefoil	Yellow/June-August	Pond edge, container	Common Blue
Greater Knapweed	Purple/July-September	Border, meadow	Many species
Hedge Cranesbill	Mauve/June-August	Border, meadow	Brimstone
Hemp Agrimony	Pink/July-September	Border, pond edge	Many species
Horseshoe Vetch	Yellow/April-July	Border, container	Common Blue
Ivy	White/September-November	Border	Red Admiral, Comma
Kidney Vetch	Yellow/June-September	Border, container	Common Blue
Lady's Smock	Mauve/April-June	Border, meadow	Green-veined White, Orange-tip
Lesser Burdock	Purple/July-September	Wild patch	Peacock, Brimstone
Meadow Cranesbill	Blue/June-September	Border, meadow	Small Tortoiseshell, Skippers
Oxeye Daisy	White/May-September	Border, meadow, container	Many species
Primrose	Yellow/March-April	Border, container	Small Tortoiseshell, Brimstone
Purple Loosestrife	Purple/June-August	Border, pond edge	Whites
Ragged Robin	Pink/May-August	Border, meadow, pond edge	Whites
Rockrose	Yellow/June-September	Border, container	Blues
Scotch Thistle	Purple/July-September	Border, wild patch	Small Tortoiseshell
Sheep's Bit	Mauve/May-August	Border, container	Many species
Small Scabious	Mauve/July-August	Border, container	Many species
Teasel	Pink/July-August	Border, wild patch	Many species
Thrift	Pink/April-August	Border, container	Small Tortoiseshell
Vervain	Pink/white/June-October	Border, wild patch	Whites
Viper's Bugloss	Purple/June-September	Border, wild patch	Skippers
Water Mint	Pink/July-September	Pond edge, container	Many species
Wild Basil	Pink/July-September	Meadow, container	Whites
Wild Marjoram	Pink/July-September	Border, meadow, container	Many species
Yarrow	White/July-October	Meadow, wild patch	Meadow Brown, Ringlet

Many species = where more than 3 species are attracted to a particular plant.

Butterfly nectar plants – garden plants

Some flowers may attract the odd butterfly, but the plants listed here are amongst the best at attracting large numbers of insects to their nectar.

Plant	Colour/Flowering Time	Best species/varieties	Favourite nectar source for..
Annuals/Biennials			
Candytuft	Various/Summer	Pale colours	Many species
Cornflower	Various/Summer	Any	Many species
Cosmos	Various/Late Summer	Early Sensation mixed	Many species
Dahlia	Various/Late Summer	Single varieties, Coltness, Redskin	Painted Lady
Heliotrope	Purple/Late Summer		Many species
Honesty	Purple, white/Late Spring		Many species
Scabious	Various/Summer	Any	Many species
Sweet Rocket	Mauve, white/Late Spring		Many species
Sweet William	Various/Late spring	Pale colours	Skippers
Sunflower	Yellow/Late Summer	Avoid very double types	Many species
Verbena	Various/Summer	Pale colours	Red Admiral
Wallflower	Various/Late Spring	Pale colours	Whites
Perennials			
Aubretia	Mauve, pink/Spring	Single varieties	Many species
Catmint	Blue/Summer	Any	Whites
Coneflower	Pink, white/Late Summer	Any	Red Admiral
Cornflower	Blue, purple/Summer	*Centaurea* species	Many species
Echinacea	Pink/Summer	Any	Many species
Fleabane	Pink, mauve/Summer	Erigeron varieties	Small Tortoiseshell
Globe Thistle	Blue/Summer		Many species
Heather	Pink, purple/Summer		Comma, small copper
Hyssop	Blue, white/Summer		Whites
Ice Plant	Pink, white/Late Summer	Pale colours preferred	Many species
Knapweed	Pink, purple/Summer	*Centaurea dealbata*	
Lavender	Purple/Summer	Any varieties including dwarf	Many species
Marjoram	Pink/Summer	Any	Many species
Michaelmas Daisy	Various/Late Summer	Single, pale varieties	Many species
Mint	Pink/Summer	Any	Many species
Phlox	Various/Summer	*Phlox paniculata*, pale colours	Many species
Scabious	Various/Summer	Any	Many species
Sneezeweed	Various/Late Summer	*Helenium* species	Red admiral
Thyme	Pink/Summer	Any	Many species
Valerian	Pink, white, red/ Summer	Pink and white varieties	Many species
Verbena	Various/Summer	*Verbena bonariensis*	Many species
Wallflower	Various/Summer	Bowles mauve	Whites
Shrubs			
Buddleia davidii	Mauve, white/Summer	Pale colours especially Lochinch	Many species
Buddleia weyeriana	Yellow/July-November	Any	Many species
Escallonia	Various/Summer	White varieties	Holly blue
Goat willow	Yellow/Spring		Small Tortoiseshell, Peacock
Hebe	Pale colours/Summer-Autumn	Pink varieties, Great Orme	Many species
Privet	White/Summer	Wild species	Many species
Wild Plum	White/Spring		Peacock, Small Tortoiseshell

Many species = where more than 3 species are attracted to a particular plant.

Some larval food plants for garden butterflies

Species	Larval Food Plants	Location in the Garden
Brimstone	Alder Buckthorn and Purging Buckthorn	Border, hedgerow
Comma	Nettles, Hops, Elm	Container, wild patch
Common Blue	Bird's-foot Trefoil, Restharrow, Black Medick	Border, meadow, container
Essex Skipper	Various grasses	Meadow, wild patch
Gatekeeper	Native meadow grasses, especially Fescues, Cock's-foot and Bents	Meadow, wild patch
Green-veined White	Garlic Mustard, Sweet Rocket*, Lady's Smock	Border, meadow
Holly Blue	Holly, Ivy, Dogwood	Hedgerow
Large Skipper	Native grasses, especially Cock's-foot and False Brome	Meadow, wild patch
Large White	Many *Brassica* species (cabbages), Nasturtiums*	Border, container
Marbled White	Native grasses, especially Fescues, Cock's-foot	Meadow, wild patch
Meadow Brown	Native meadow grasses especially Bents	Meadow, wild patch
Orange-tip	Garlic Mustard, Sweet Rocket*, Lady's Smock, Honesty*	Border, meadow
Painted Lady	Thistles, Mallow	Container, wild patch
Peacock	Nettles	Container, wild patch
Red Admiral	Nettles	Container, wild patch
Ringlet	Native grasses, especially Cock's-foot, False Brome, Annual Meadow Grass	Meadow, wild patch
Small Copper	Wild Sorrel	Border, meadow, container
Small Skipper	Native grasses, especially Yorkshire Fog, Timothy and False Brome	Meadow, wild patch
Small Tortoiseshell	Nettles	Container, wild patch
Small White	All *Brassica* species, Nasturtiums*	Border, container
Speckled Wood	Native meadow grasses, especially Cock's-foot, False Brome and Couch Grass	Meadow, wild patch
Wall Brown	Native meadow grasses, especially Cock's-foot, Common Bent and Yorkshire Fog	Meadow, wild patch

* non-native plants

Some meadow grasses used by butterflies

Bents	*Agrostis* species	Meadow Grass	*Poa* species
Cock's-foot	*Dactylis glomerata*	Timothy	*Phleum pratense*
Couch	*Elymus* species	Tor Grass	*Brachypodium pinnatum*
False Brome	*Brachypodium sylvaticum*	Yorkshire Fog	*Holcus lanatus*
Fescue	*Festuca* species		

Native shrubs for a butterfly hedge

Shrub		Notes
Blackthorn	*Prunus spinosa*	Nectar for spring Small Tortoiseshells and Peacocks
Buckthorn	*Frangula alnus* or *Rhamnus cathartica*	Larval food plant of Brimstone
Dogwood	*Cornus sanguinea*	Alternative larval food plant for Holly Blue
Goat Willow	*Salix caprea*	Nectar source for spring Small Tortoiseshells and Peacocks and a fantastic larval food plant for moths
Hawthorn	*Crataegus monogyna*	Good shelter and food for wildlife
Holly	*Ilex aquifolium*	Excellent shelter, and larval food plant of Holly Blue
Wild Plum	*Prunus* spp.	Early nectar source for Small Tortoiseshells and Peacocks
Wild Privet	*Ligustrum vulgare*	Good nectar source

The Garden Butterfly Year

The table shows the months that you are most likely to see the most common garden butterflies plus a few migrant or more unusual species. The time period will vary depending on where in the country you are situated and the weather conditions, and butterflies will sometimes be seen outside these times.

Species	J	F	M	A	M	J	J	A	S	O	N	D
Brimstone			🦋	🦋	🦋	🦋	🦋	🦋	🦋			
Clouded Yellow						🦋	🦋	🦋	🦋			
Comma				🦋			🦋	🦋	🦋			
Common Blue					🦋	🦋		🦋	🦋			
Essex Skipper							🦋	🦋				
Gatekeeper							🦋	🦋				
Green Hairstreak					🦋	🦋						
Green-veined White					🦋	🦋	🦋	🦋				
Holly Blue				🦋	🦋		🦋	🦋				
Large Skipper						🦋	🦋	🦋				
Large White					🦋	🦋	🦋	🦋				
Marbled White						🦋	🦋	🦋				
Meadow Brown						🦋	🦋	🦋	🦋			
Orange-tip				🦋	🦋	🦋						
Painted Lady				🦋	🦋	🦋	🦋	🦋	🦋			
Peacock				🦋	🦋		🦋	🦋	🦋			
Red Admiral				🦋	🦋	🦋	🦋	🦋	🦋	🦋		
Ringlet						🦋	🦋					
Small Copper					🦋	🦋	🦋	🦋	🦋			
Small Skipper							🦋	🦋				
Small Tortoiseshell				🦋	🦋	🦋	🦋	🦋	🦋			
Small White				🦋	🦋	🦋	🦋	🦋	🦋			
Speckled Wood				🦋	🦋	🦋	🦋	🦋	🦋			
Wall Brown					🦋	🦋	🦋	🦋				

Other nature books by Brambleby Books

Making Garden Meadows – How to create a natural haven for wildlife
Jenny Steel
ISBN 978 1908241 221

Norfolk Wildlife – A Calendar and Site Guide
Adrian M. Riley
ISBN 978 1908241 047

British and Irish Butterflies
Adrian M. Riley
ISBN 978 0955392 801

Bird Words – Poetic images of wild birds
Hugh D. Loxdale
ISBN 978 0954334 734

*Garden Photo Shoot –
A Photographer's Yearbook of Garden Wildlife*
John Thurlbourn
ISBN 978 0955392 832

Walking with Birds
Colin Whittle
ISBN 978 1908241 351

*Buzzing!
Discover the poetry in garden minibeasts*
Anneliese Emmans Dean
ISBN 978 1908241 443

*Sheer Cliffs and Shearwaters –
A Skomer Island Journal*
Richard Kipling
ISBN 978 1908241 214

*The Wild Flowers of the Isles of Purbeck,
Brownsea and Sandbank 2ed.*
Edward Pratt
ISBN 9781908241 450

The Wild Flowers of Jersey
Deirdre Shirreffs
ISBN 9781908241 337

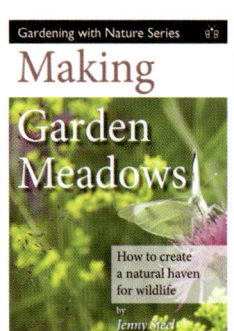
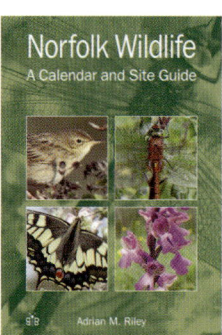
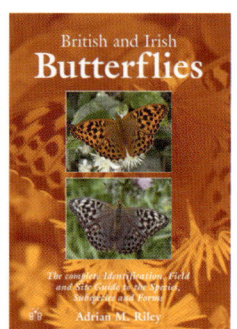

www.bramblebybooks.co.uk